IF I COULD TURN BACK THE HANDS OF TIME . . .

IF I COULD TURN BACK THE HANDS OF TIME . . .

SIMON M. MATLOU

AuthorHouse™
1663 Liberty Drive
Bloomington, IN 47403
www.authorhouse.com
Phone: 1-800-839-8640

Published by AuthorHouse   11/13/2012

ISBN: 978-1-4772-3911-7 (sc)
ISBN: 978-1-4772-3912-4 (e)

I would like to thank all the people who supported me by purchasing the above book, BEYOND THE HORIZON which is my first book published in 2011. This book can be purchased on line in recognized bookshops across the globe.

DEDICATION

My warm thanks to my wife Thoko Mirriam and our children Lesego Romeo and Amanda Tshegofatso for their support and unfailing love, my parents Mr Frans and Mrs Tinah Matlou for being there for me in difficult times, not forgetting my brothers Frank, Paul, Lucas, Gideon and sisters Paulinah and Magdeline.Credit is due to my nephew Andrew and my niece Mmapula. Special tribute goes to my Creator for giving me strength and protection.

CONTENTS

Photo : Tshegofatso Amanda

Simon M. Matlou

IF I COULD TURN BACK THE HANDS OF TIME . . . .

If I could turn back the hands of time,
To sight of green grass and colourful flowers nod together,
In warm, quiet and friendly whisper in the midday breeze,
The language I could clearly treasure and understand,
Under the verdant branches in the veldt where I used to play.

If I could turn back the hands of time,
To melancholy songs of the cuckoo birds,
To the bees murmuring, small birds chanting merrily,
To the sounds of water in raging rivers and streams,
And the heavy pattering rain on the zinc roof.

If I could turn back the hands of time,
To smells of steaks and chips in the passageways,
Delightful odours of plants so sweet and strong,
To home brewed beers in the over-brimming glasses,
And the golden apple green as the fridge swings open.

If I could turn back the hands of time,
And feel warm heater air caressing me in winter,
The soft touch of aircon in the sweltering atmosphere,
Sweet taste of coffee and cold drinks to relieve fatigue as the sun breaks,
That made me dream of the events before tomorrow!

I used to stretch my hands, dressed myself and went where I wanted,
But now, with my joints all aching, senses fading and eyes gradually growing dim,
I stretch out my hands and somebody dresses me up,
And leads me to where I do not want to go,
Yes, I cannot turn back the hands of time now!

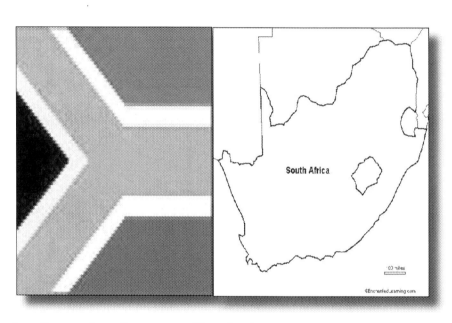

http://www.enchantedlearning.com/Home.html

Simon M. Matlou

THE WHOLE NEW WORLD

Your attention, please!
Let me tell these:
I have been to the mountain's top,
That is why I am yelling at my voice's top,
Because I have seen the Promised Land,
Our whole new world, lies clear.

Be patient, I say this with a notion!
This is a spacious place for everyone
Though we are a great multitude no one
Can count from every race to form this rainbow nation.
We have come out of great trials and tribulations
White washed in the blood of sacrifice.
Strong unity amongst us must suffice,
For this is the whole new world!

Be strong and courageous, this way please!
Get ready to cross Limpopo River into the south,
With songs of praise flowing from the mouth.
Our promised land starts from Limpopo River in the south of the north,
And extends to include all the territories till where two oceans meet,
And we as proud people will go forth,
And where we shall set our feet
Lies clearly, our whole new world!

I know we cannot contain this excitement, quiet please!
Our whole new world lies here,
To every one of us it is crystal clear!
Somebody out there, please come with a song?
I mean you over there, please Mr or Mrs?
For a new day has dawned upon us after so long!
Even though yet, we don't know the tune,
Everybody, please just play and sing along,
And we will learn the tune of this new song soon!

Photo: by Lesego Romeo

Simon M. Matlou

A THIEF STOLE MY HEART

She looked stunning—absolutely stunning!
Glowing brightly like a rose in early morning hours,
Loose-limbed, with magnetic sea-green forget-me-not eyes
That illuminated the very dark side of me,
Moreover, awakened the real man inside of me!
That was love-at-first-sight
And second-once-in-a-life-time-opportunity!

I could feel this chilly creepy sensation,
Running down the spine into the roots of my hair!
With the adrenalin pouring . . . , my heart skipped a beat . . . ,
I gasped for air, for there was too much love—
Real love comes shooting through my veins!
I could notice her beauty shining brightly
When her broad sheepish smile began!

She was as different to other women
Encountered before as a whisky is to water!
The difference between the two of them
Is that one provides a kick—really a horse kick!
I felt like following her like a shadow
By her side wherever she went
Because that thief stole my heart away!

The third Summer had come upon me,
She was still playing in my dreams,
Reverberating in my mind in a continuous blast.
"Fight this weakness out or burn with passion,
Why not now, chap, where do you stand now?"
My friend pointed this out to me repeatedly!
To arrive at that hospital, to find that she has been transferred?

Photo: Boitumelo Mamma Matlou

WE HAVE ONCE WALKED HERE IN THE DAWN OF TIME

The day we die a soft breeze will wipe out our footprints in the sand,
And when the wind dies down, who will tell the timelessness
That once we walked this way in the dawn of time? [1]
Who is going to tell this generation and the next
That we have once walked here in the dawn of time?
But before the sun finally sets on me, please hear this:

When the first sunrays beamed across Mmapela in Polokwane,
We stood at the end of the rainbow watching and admiring its beauty.
When we lifted our sights far into the distant horizon,
We realized that the sun, moon, fire, water
And stars of heaven were all the gifts we had,
When we walked here in the dawn of time.

We flew on the wings of an eagle, and soared high above the clouds,
We admired the beauty of wild flowers of the impressive Seabe Village,
The grey sands of Lepaaku Village, the soil-coloured waters of Moutse River.
Observed how hyenas, wild dogs and leopards beneath the vast Hammanskraal's sky,
Trembled in fear and surrendered the stage to the fearsome mighty lions,
When we walked here in the dawn of time!

We stilled the tidal waves and quietened the prevailing storms,
To exercise domination in the depths of the forever—roaring oceans,
So that the wondrous herrings, tunas, dolphins, seals and the fierce sharks
Could thrive and survive together in perfect harmony in the same deep blue waters,
Amongst the trenches, coral reefs, mountain ranges and pebbles of the ocean beds
When we walked here in the dawn of time.

We rode the whirlwind; we silenced the forever-rumbling thunder,
We steered the clouds and our attitudes determined the day's weather!
We hovered above the expanses of our land, seas and the skies to guide the rains.
We skated through the glaciers, snows, frosts and the ever—changing seasons,
And our footsteps shaped this land, its valleys, mountains, rivers and the glades!
Look at our footprints here in the sand; we have once walked here in the dawn of time!

---

[1] From Bushman's song: Mrs Coral Fourie

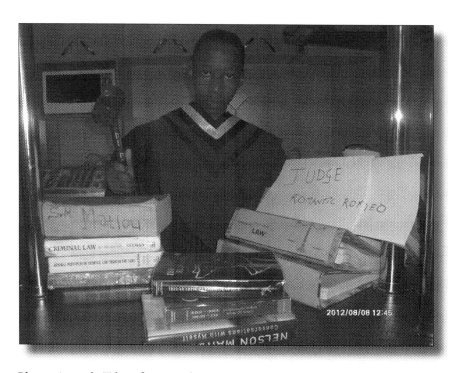

Photo: Amanda Tshegofatso Matlou

Simon M. Matlou

GUILTY AS CHARGED!

Justice Romantic Romeo: Stand up in court!

Case No 345/03/2012

Accused: Ms Provocative Dishonest

Address: 197 Mpopotwane Street

Sun Valley, Mamelodi West

0122

(1)　PARTICULARS OF CHARGES

(1)　Charge 1: Sweeping my heart away.

(1)(a)　Alternative charge to charge 1: Stealing away my soul.

(2)　Charge 2: Provocatively hijacking my feelings.

(2)(a)　Alternative charge to charge 2: Playing continuously in my dreams.

In terms of the Constitution's Bill of Rights and Ubuntu Regulations 14(3) that reads with Batho-Pele Principles and Corporate Governance Regulations 18(3),

You performed an act that constituted an offence and you therefore stand accused of:

Unlawfully and intentionally sweeping my heart away on 2012/03/16 at 16:00, On my birthday, on Sunday at 197 Mpopotwane Street, Sun Valley in Mamelodi West, and alternatively stealing my soul on that day, time and place.

AND FURTHER . . . .

You unlawfully and intentionally, provocatively hijacked my feelings in broad daylight, in full view of the people, and alternatively played continuously in my dreams every 12:00 midnight from that day until present!

(2)　PLEADING:

Justice Romantic Romeo: How do you plead Mrs Provocative Dishonest? Guilty or not guilty?

Ms Provocative Dishonest: Eh . . . . eh . . . . guilty, my Worship !

(3) FINDINGS:

Justice Romantic Romeo: Guilty as charged! Guilty on all the charges!

(4) SENTENCE:

Justice Romantic Romeo: Since you pleaded guilty to all the charges, I will slap you with this light sentence:

(1) Be the apple of my eye and my lover for life!
(2) With NO PAROLE and NO LEAVE TO APPEAL for this sentence, be the keeper of my dreams!

(5) COURT ADJOURNS:

Justice Romantic Romeo: All stand up in court !The court is adjourned, And we will live happily ever after.

Photo : Thoko Merriam

THE SECRET RIVER

There is a vein of life in the thicket,
Secretly making the ground green,
To teem with plantation so verdant,
Matures fruits to ripeness and flowers to blossom,
Despite that, remains unnoticed from some people!

This is the long broad Secret River,
It flows down from its mountain source,
It rushes and winds around the curve,
It diverges into two and leaves a triangular island,
Right in the middle of the gentle brimming stream.

Where shadows dive from the sun-baked mountain top,
In the ever whirling soil coloured pool,
Upon the bubbling water, amongst the hollow stones,
Appear thirty-nine doves, all paired but one!
Amazingly, so fascinating, their hearts have not grown old!

There is a slow moon rising on the Secret River,
Shines brightly in the tranquil clear water at dusk,
With clear broad sweep of gentle wind howling,
And the cold air rustling through forest trees and leaves!

When the only tips of the horns of cattle,
Are seen etched against the morning sky of Seabe Village,
Followed by the sunrise to banish the darkness of the night,
Women are seen in long files from the Secret River,
With buckets of water gracefully balanced on their heads!

Photo :NASA: Creative Commons Licensing

IF YOU THINK GOD
DOES NOT EXIST . . . .

If you think God does not exist,
Take a look at the beginning of life, the miracle of birth, the greatest mystery:[2]
The incredible brain power, the home of great ideas, emotions and imaginations,
To register and process all signals and information outclassing the latest computer!
Lungs, the breath of life and ears the masterpiece of sonic engineering,
Eyes, the miracle of sight and hands the secret of human success,
The heart, the powerhouse of the body and kidneys the waste disposal,
The transport of oxygen and all nutrients all over the body.
The touch, the sense of feeling, and the blood circulatory system,
The genetic print of the DNA, the replication of all our information,
And systems of other organs that co-ordinate without our conscious efforts,
Processing all kinds of food we put in our mouths without our intervention!

If you think, God does not exist,
You better look around you!
Take a walk at night and look up at beautiful stars,
As they bedeck the good Heavens like swinging magic torches.
Look at the solar system, which is becoming increasingly complex,
With other, heavenly bodies revolving around the sun and other planetary satellites,
With galaxy of stars called the Milky Way consisting of hundred billion stars.
These heavenly bodies are so reliable in their rotation day and night,
Century after century with complete accuracy matching our modern times.[3]
Look at the sun, as it rises and sets and hurries back to where it rises,
All rivers flow into sea and yet the sea is not full,
Oh, what a wonderful universe that we live in!

If you still think, that God does not exist,
Take a deep breath and look around you!
Better look at this universe that has been designed for you habitation,
With the earth and other planets revolving around the sun and their moons,

---

[2]   Steele P. Encyclopaedia of Animal Life and

[3]   Watch Tower Publications

Making our days, nights, weeks, months, seasons, and years possible.
Look at the atmosphere with mixture of gases to enable us to breath,
Variety of coloured flowers with sweet scents to delight us,
Variety of food so delicious to enjoy,
Forests, mountains, lakes, rivers and other beautiful creations to view,
Beautiful sunrises and sunsets to enhance our enjoyments.
This beautiful universe we are living in owe its existence
To the invisible controlling intelligent powerful force—that is God!

Photo: Thoko Merriam

Simon M. Matlou

RATHER BE GENTLE
TO THE GROWING MINDS

I believe the children are our treasure,
We rather be gentle to these growing minds to build their future,
We must treat them with kindness and loving care,
Children need to loved and guided, every parent must be aware!

Children should be afforded the opportunity to grow
Up in an environment that free from fear
And receive education in an atmosphere
Free from violence and disorder, which every parent must know!

Their childhood should be of discovery and peace of playing,
Joy, happiness, learning, hopefulness and growing.
This is their time to tie close bonds and relation
With their families and friends to build the nation.

Children are dependent, vulnerable and full of innocence,
They should be given a sense of pride and motivation.
Their future should be shaped in harmony and co-operation,
As they mature and gain new experience.

All children have legitimate claim to family care,
To basic right to nutrition, shelter and not be left bare.
They are entitled to protection from abuse and insecurity,
And finally to be treated with respect and dignity.

I believe all the children are our future,
They look up to us as adults to protect and nurture,
But on the contrary, they continue to experience multiplicity of violations,
An increasing epidemic eating away our society and this rainbow nation!

Photo: Lesego Romeeo

Simon M. Matlou

THE MOST WANTED CRIMINAL
YOU KNOW

He does crime before you,
And yet you keep quiet,
He resides amongst you,
He tells you he is from a poor background,
And that is not a licence to commit crime,
He is the most wanted criminal, don't you know that?

He is a robber,
He is currently in your midst,
He has once worked for the Security Forces,
But now he has been dismissed,
Because he was involved in a number of cash-in-transit robberies,
And he has escaped from prison, don't you know?

She is a fraudster,
You know that fully well,
She was once employed by the Computer Company,
Her employers could not take it any longer,
Because she defrauded them millions of rands,
She is on the run, don't you know?

He is a well-known hijacker,
You see him every day,
He has a fleet of expensive cars,
And you know he was never employed before,
He always spins tyres of stolen vehicles in your area,
He is still evading justice, don't you know?

She is a drug lord,
She thinks, she is a role model for the kids,
She owns strings of mansions in the affluent suburbs,
You know fully well that she becomes active at night,

And that she corroborates well with some members of the police service,
That's why she thinks is untouchable, don't you know that?

He is a murderer,
He is your father, son, cousin
Uncle, brother, grandfather or your son-in-law,
He showers your daughter, aunt or sister with the most expensive gifts,
And you provide refuge to him,
Harbouring a criminal is crime, don't you know that?

She is a burglar in your area,
You help her sustain her market,
Because she sells those stolen articles to you,
You know her hide out,
And most importantly where she hides those stolen articles,
Buying stolen articles is crime, don't you know that?

Gentle communities out there, we are sick and tired of crime,
Let's join hands together and flush out these criminals,
We know them and we are certain they are in minority,
Let us join hands together and make their lives a hell where they live!
Just call 10111 or 0860010111 to name and shame them!
Give only their names and not your name, don't you know that?

Photo: Amanda Tshegofatso

I HAVE A DREAM

All over the world, we all dream,
But we do not dream equally.
We all yearn for and have desperation, motivation
And courage to make our dreams come true.
But others wake up to find their dreams empty of significance
The future belongs to those who see beauty in their dreams! [4]

Gerald Alston of the Manhattans had a dream,
He dreamt of peace all over the world.
Martin Luther King had a dream.
In spite of difficulties and frustration of those moments,
He dreamt that Mississippi state, sweltering with heat of oppression,
Would be transformed into an oasis of freedom, peace and justice.

I have a dream too!
I see South Africa as a safe and secured environment,
Where its inhabitants pursue their daily lives in peace and safety,
Free from the fear of crime and violence where they walk and live,
South Africans being a society in which fundamental rights
Of our senior citizens, women and children are protected.

I see all South Africans enjoying peace and tranquillity of their homes,
Senior citizens, women and children walking peacefully on the streets,
Enjoying their walking, shopping and their entertainments,
Women going and coming to work and dressing as they like,
In their environments shaped in harmony and co-operation
Without fear, that limit the enjoyments of their lives!

South Africa shall be a safe and a well secured environment,
Where we will enjoy the pleasure of watching our children
Enjoying the joy and peace of playing, learning and growing,
A warm embrace from someone we love
And a hearty laughter during a good meal with friends.
We are almost there!

---

[4]   Nelson Mandela Speech

Simon M. Matlou

Photo : Department of Trade and Industry and Tourism

SCENES FROM THE SOUTH SIDE

The yellow sun moves slowly up the blue skies,
The cold morning air traps and distributes light evenly,
That every living entity can wake up to this inspiring sense of awe;
Colourful flowers in joyous mood, under verdant branches,
Nod together in their warm and quiet conversation,
As bees buzz and small birds chant merrily,
We feel confronted by the beauty of nature!

Not so far away, swallows encircle in the air,
Pigeons in commemoration fly in their intact rings,
Ravens gently glide above the mountain high
As the eagle takes a flight beyond the horizon!
Full-grown lambs leap and cicadas sing madly,
Penguins flap their wings continuously!

Trailing with colours of the New South African flag
Roars six Impala aircrafts emitting grey smoke,
As the proud strong rainbow nation, hold back the tears of joy!
The new head of state beams with pride in a brilliant sunshine,
To the endless roars of masses below at the Union Buildings,
As Nkosi—Sikelele—Africa echoes with the force that can light the nighty skies!

As shadows move slowly across the earth's surface,
Millions of twinkling points of light flicker in joyous assembly,
Some faint, others much brighter like swinging torches of eternity,
Others, steady and constant but still adorning the good heavens and earth!
A band of emitted light stretches across the nighty skies, for
Freedom has just arrived in South Africa,—oh, what a day!
Freedom to exist, to expression, to dignity and finally to vote!

Photo : Lesego Romeo

I WILL NEVER SEE THEM AGAIN

"Abide with me . . . , as the darkness deepens,
When earth's joy grows dim . . . , its glory passes away,
Through darkness and sunshine . . . , oh, abide with me!" [5]
Repeatedly invoking the grace of God to wash away pains and sorrows,
And also harmonizing in the background with the force that illuminated
The nighty skies echoed this hymn, sounds of instruments and drums!
I will never see those slain guardians of law again,
To share those precious moments,
Like we used to do in the living years!

In that sweltering evening atmosphere,
Police officers in uniform had to hold back tears while saluting,
When widowed spouses, children, colleagues
And parents of police officers laid wreaths to honour
Their loved ones who laid down their lives protecting ours,
In honour of their call to serve and protect us.
I will never see them again,
To share those precious moments,
Like we always used to do in the living years!

Four South African Police Service helicopters carrying the National Flags,
Hovered above the Union Building, as the Police Code of Conduct,
Was acknowledged by the Minister of Police, a sign of
Selflessness of the police officers, who died on line of duty,
And a pledge by all who live on (a norm in the South African Police Services!)
But how much longer do we have to see these guardians of law murdered this way?
I will never see them again,
To share those precious moments
Like we used to do in the living years!

---

[5]   Servamus Policing Magazize 1998 and

As the flag was flown at half-mast at the Union Building [6]
All stood up motionless, their eyes directed at the flag,
Amid the deafening silence of the evening atmosphere,
Some sighed, sounds of grief audible, tears oozed
From some of the friends, family members and colleagues,
Thinking of hardships of living without their loved ones.
I will never see them again,
To share those precious moments
Like we used to do in the living years!

Mixed emotions were invoked as friends and family members
Of the deceased were finally walked the red carpet,
In honour and respect, as others` bright shining pride
Lit up the Union Building, others sobbed with great grief,
Despair and deep sorrow during this moving ceremony,
The South African Police Service Commemoration day!
I will never see them again,
To share those precious moments
Like we always used to do in the living years!

Photo: Creative Commons Licensing

Simon M. Matlou

DEATH

Some call death mighty, fearful
Dreadful and ultimate victory over life.
For some, death entered humankind through Adam
And then reigned till present.

Some refer to death as cessation
Of all the function of life;
Stopping of heartbeat, breathing, brain activity
And functions of body cells.

Some refer to death as your identical twin,
To walk side by side and hand in hand,
To inflict physical and emotional pain, if he so desires,
In addition, to rob people of you, their love ones!

I refer to death as the most comfortable vehicle,
For the continuation of life into another world,
A path we must all trot
If we would ever want to come to our Maker!

When pharynx, larynx or windpipe is blocked,
Body completely immersed in water,
Excessive force applied to damage tissues badly,
And too much blood oozing from severely cut wounds, we pass away!

Though we all yearn for longevity,
There is a natural or unnatural inherent limit to life!
Our last enemy to also die is death,
When finally death will be swallowed in victory!

Photo : Creative Commons Licensing

Simon M. Matlou

I AM HIV/AIDS

Saint Luke predicted me long time ago,
While the Book of Revelation warned you about me.
I am raging like a wild fire,
I am growling like a lion,
I have spotted you and I will pounce on you!
I am HIV/AIDS!

I attack people in all socio-economic and educational classes,
I cut across cultural and religious sects,
Graves and hospitals bear this testimony.
Despite significant medical accomplishments,
I remain incurable,
I am HIV/AIDS

From Africa to America, Australia to Asia and Artantica to Europe.
From Cape Provinces to Limpopo and Mpumalanga to Kwa-Zulu / Natal.
From Bekkersdal to Grobblersdal and Makapanstad to Marabastad.
From Sun Valley to Sun City and Mamelodi to Mametlhake.
From Witlagte to Langlagte and Suiwerskuil to Kromkuil.
I am reigning, I am HIV/AIDS.

Woe for the earth and for the sea,
Because I have descended in great anger to devour you!
I refer to you, who do not abstain,
I mean you there, who are not faithful,
And you here who do not condomise,
For I am HIV/AIDS.

Media has warned you,
Priests have preached at the top of their voices,
Politicians have cried loud,
Organizations and institutions have given you warnings,
But all these have come to naught,
Now I will kill you like flies, for I am HIV/AIDS

This is not news to you,
You will certainly catch me through unprotected sex,
Shared infected needles and syringes, contaminated blood,
And from an infected mother to her unborn child.
I then multiply in your blood, mercilessly attacking
Your defence system and leave you for the dead,
For I am HIV/AIDS.

You know this fully well;
You cannot catch me through
Sneezing, sharing toilet seats, coughing,
Or shaking hands with an infected person.
Behold, even if you are not infected,
You are affected by me, for I am HIV/AIDS.

Even though I am dreadful and mighty,
I will finally die and my heart is sore,
That will be when sense is finally knocked in your head,
That will be when you abstain from sex,
You remain faithful to your partner or condomise,
Remember, prevention is better than cure, for I am HIV/AIDS!

Simon M. Matlou

Photo: NASA : Creative Commons Licensing

MY ZERO HOUR

Grieving voices of people out of vision in limbo,
Weeping of people in great pain audible too,
Whilst at the end of the rainbow, all glowing in white,
Faithful subjects sing with a force that can light the skies!

When the dark clouds finally descend upon me,
I will know my zero hour has come,
And when the sun no longer shines for me,
I know I will meet my fate beyond the blue!

Here I am, standing on the threshold,
Those I persecuted, please forgive me,
For those I guarded, surely I protected!
Laws I transgressed, I thought I was above!

Simon M. Matlou

Photo: Zulu M

WELCOME TO THE
REAL WORLD, GUYS

Welcome to the real world, guys!

South Africa salutes you this evening, because you made her proud!

You are very fortunate to be bestowed upon, that honour of serving and protecting our citizens,

You are now a new breed of people forming a larger part of law enforcement.

This evening belongs to you, matured men and women glowing brightly in dignified blue!

Having endured a lot during training, you have graduated from childhood to face the real world out there,

Where crime and evil sometimes seem to completely outweigh the good and the kind.

There will be times when you would firmly believe that God no longer cares,

When your emotions will be confused and your hope pulled down in whirlpool of despair.

Welcome to the real world, guys!

You will sometimes find yourselves being caught up in the cross fire between different sections of the community,

Nevertheless, continue to be impartial, more gentler and friendlier in the manner you deal with those communities.

The public out there have high expectations from you,

They want to see you catch criminals,

Reducing levels of crime that is visible and retaining

The control of streets on behalf and concerns of law-abiding citizens.

These challenges have become increasingly complex and demanding

Requiring endurance, patience, skills and high levels of professionalism.

Welcome to the real world, guys !

You will sometimes be expected to trod where even the angels are afraid to trot,

You will be faced with variety of tasks and challenges daily,

Such as intensive patrols, attending crime scenes,

Taking statements, checking records, making enquiries,

Referring people to appropriate support services,

Dealing with public and general administration of your station,
And assuring public confidence to go out on safer streets.
While exercising those duties, have and display absolute dedication to those important tasks,
And never undermine authority and discipline!

Welcome to the real world, guys!
This passing out parade this evening is an important milestone,
Marking the beginning of your demanding and challenging career.
Remember policing is not just a job,
It is a vacation, a calling you did not deny.
This should be your absolute motivating factor.
Be tough and have no-nonsense approach to criminals,
While adhering to high ethical values and morals.
Resist temptations and live in accordance with the Police Code of Conduct,
Cultivate respect for law in both your personal and professional lives!

Photo: Ushaka Photographer, KZN

Simon M. Matlou

TRIALS OF LIFE

Life is a beautiful thing,
It is man's precious gift,
Life gives man chance to love, work and play,
And it is meant to be lived to the full.

Life has its up and downs,
Because it goes round and round in circles.
Life can sometimes get you down
That's why it takes some practice to get it under control!

Life can be colder than you know,
And amazingly throws you a curve,
And become too much to take,
And sometimes just disappear.

Trials of life are not meant to make you despair,
But to see how far you can fly,
With all its minuses and broken dreams,
It is still our beautiful life!

Photo :NASA: Creative Commons Licensing

Simon M. Matlou

DEDICATION TO
HEAVENLY BODIES

From our observation platform, the planet earth,
Which is many million kilometres from the sun,
A vast globe of metal weighing about billion tons,
Coated with rock, to give its present conditions of life,
Spinning on its axis around the sun between Venus and Mars,
Wheeled through space many kilometres per hour,
Carrying more than thousand million human passengers,
As well as other living organisms too numerous to count,
Completing its journey in three hundred and sixty five days,
Five hours, forty eight minutes and forty six seconds,
We are able to observe other heavenly bodies termed planets
In procession from our observation stage, the earth!

Our stars are other celestial bodies appearing as luminous objects,
In the nighty sky, so far from the earth, those are vast gases,
With temperatures hotter than that of the sun,
And more than hundred million degrees in the interior.
All those heavenly bodies of the universe are evenly spread [5]
In some sort of unity and they emit an awe-inspiring band of light
Known as the Milky Way, rotating in such a way that all of its stars
Are revolving at different speeds around the centre.
All appear like republics controlling one another movements,
In a space held together by the gravitational attraction,
Indistinguishable to the naked eye encircling our good heavens!

The sun, the star around which the earth orbits,
And from which the earth receive its light and warmth,
It is a ball of fire blazing violently with countless hydrogen.
The moon, a natural satellite of the earth so many kilometres from the earth,
Orbits the earth monthly, illuminated by the sun, travelling at one kilometre per second!
Meteors become incandescent, because of friction from the atmosphere,
The comet, composed of ice and dust is surrounded by gas, with its tail,

Pointing from the sun, it is a hazy object orbiting our sun too !
Asteroids are lumps of rocky materials ranging in size,
From particles to mini-planets each travelling in its own particular orbit,
But majority keeping within a wide belt between planets Mars and Jupiter!

The Mercury, termed the Greek's Fleet Manager of Gods, it is the first planet from the sun,[7]
The Venus, termed the Greek's Goddess of Love and Beauty, it is second from the sun,
Mars, the reddish planet, termed the Greek's God of War, because of its colour,
It is the fourth planet from the sun and next beyond the earth.
Jupiter, the largest planet enough to hold thousand earths, it is the fifth from the sun,
It is termed the Greek's Lord of Heavens and presumed father of Gods and Men.
Saturn, the sixth from the sun, it has a system of broad flat rings,
And it is the coldest planet permanently covered in cloud of gases.
The Uranus, the seventh from the sun, takes eighty-four earthly years to rotate the sun!
Neptune, the eighth from the sun, takes one hundred and sixty five earthly years to rotate the sun!
Pluto, the Greek's god of the under world, it is the outermost and the most distant planet in the solar system!

---

[7]   Readers Digest: Did you know?

Photo: Simon M Matlou

THE ROUTE LESS TAKEN

The boat sailed peacefully through the silent water,
And to me that did not matter,
It looked fascinating and inviting,
All on board were warm hearted and exciting!

The river suddenly forked into two
It was pity; we had to decide on one,
As a traveller, I made my choice too,
But the majority who ruled on that day, won!

Suddenly, it all started to matter,
When caught up in the raging water,
Sending us twenty metres down the waterfall,
In the barren with no one to call.

Long time ago, I followed a route less taken,
For I was all mistaken,
I went with the flow and followed the masses,
And alas, that brought all the difference!

Simon M. Matlou

ACKNOWLEDGEMENTS

Acknowledgement is made to the following for the use of works which are their copyright:

1   Amanda Tshegofatso: *Photo's on pages 5,13,15 and 25*
2.   Creative Common Licensing: Photosfree.com: *Photo's on pages 32 and 34*
3.   Department of Trade and Industry and Tourism: *Photo on page 27*
4.   Enchantedlearning.com/Home html: *Photo on page 7*
5.   Fourie, C, 1994. *Living Legend of dying Culture. Bushman's myths, legends and fables, Sigma Press*
6.   Lesego Romeo: Photo's on pages 9, 22 and 29
7.   Mandela, N. Extract from his Speeches
8.   McCabe, J. *Wonders of the stars. Encyclopaedia of Knowledge, Volume 2*
9.   NASA: Creative Commons Licencing, Photosfree.com. *Photo's on pages 18, 37 and 44*
10.   Reader's Digest, 1990. Did you know? Partnaires Brun, Maury, France
11.   Simon M Matlou. Photo on page 47
12.   Servamus Policing Magazine, 1998
13.   South African Police Services Journal, 1999
14.   Steele, P. *Encyclopaedia of animal life*
15.   Thoko Mirriam.: *Photo's on pages 16 and 20*
16.   Ushaka Photographer, KZN: *Photo on page 42*
17.   Watch Tower Publication. *Who is God?*
18.   www.free-photos.biz/- United States (Free pictures / photographs / images / pics / photos for commercial and personal use. Public domain, royalty-free, GPL, Creative Commons pictures. Free Photos of Nature - Free Photos of People - Photos of Transportation) Date: 2012/09/29 (No permission is required to use the photo's on this website)
19.   Zulu M: *Photo on page 39*

While every effort has been made to trace and acknowledge copyright holders, for permission to use their work, this might have not been possible in a very few cases. Should any infringement have occurred, the copyright holders are invited to get in touch with the publisher, who will amend their omissions accordingly in the event of reprint

Printed in the United States
By Bookmasters